The Tennis Lover's Book of Wisdom

The Tennis Lover's Book of Wisdom

Common Sense and Uncommon Genius
From the Game's Greatest Legends

Compiled and Edited by Criswell Freeman

WALNUT GROVE PRESS
Nashville, TN 37205

ISBN 1-887655-36-0

The ideas expressed in this book are not, in all cases, exact quotations, as some have been edited for clarity and brevity. In all cases, the author has attempted to maintain the speaker's original intent. In some cases, material for this book was obtained from secondary sources, primarily print media. While every effort was made to ensure the accuracy of these sources, the accuracy cannot be guaranteed. For additions, deletions, corrections or clarifications in future editions of this text, please write WALNUT GROVE PRESS.

Printed in the United States of America
Cover Design by Mary Mazer
Typesetting & Page Layout by Sue Gerdes
Editor for Walnut Grove Press: Alan Ross
3 4 5 6 7 8 9 10 •   99 00 01

ACKNOWLEDGMENTS
The author gratefully acknowledges the helpful support of Angela Beasley, Dick and Mary Freeman, Mary Susan Freeman, and Jim Gallery.

For Don Pippen

Table of Contents

Introduction 13
Chapter 1:   The Game 15
Chapter 2:   The Mental Game 23
Chapter 3:   Practice 39
Chapter 4:   Concentration 57
Chapter 5:   The Serve 69
Chapter 6:   Strokes 79
Chapter 7:   Strategy 91
Chapter 8:   Winning and Losing 103
Chapter 9:   Life 115
Chapter 10: All-Purpose Advice 123
Chapter 11: Observations 135
Sources 149

Introduction

Every tennis match is a contest not just of skill, but of will. Thus the game's greatest players are more than finely-tuned athletes; they are also grand masters in the venerable art of gamesmanship. This book of tennis quotations unlocks their secrets.

At its best, tennis teaches us about discipline, preparation, mental toughness, and strategy. Once learned, these lessons are more valuable off the court than on.

On the pages that follow, great teachers and players share their insights on serves, strokes and strategies. You're invited to take a lesson.

1

The Game

Billie Jean King once confessed, "The game has a hold on my soul." Spoken like a true fanatic.

The ancient and respectable game of tennis takes only a few minutes to learn, but a lifetime to master. Perhaps this helps explain our undying fascination with the sport. The true fan, while never achieving the perfect match, secretly hopes for the day when each and every shot is a winner. Of course that day never comes, but the tennis lover, smitten by the sport, keeps coming back, just in case.

If you, like Billie Jean, can't get enough of that little bouncing ball, consider the quotations that follow. But be forewarned: Tennis fever, once acquired, can last a lifetime.

I want to play tennis for the right reason.
The right reason is because I love the game.

Monica Seles

We're playing a sport. A lot of times, guys
forget it's a game. That's not how it should be;
it should be fun.

Yannick Noah

You can have a good time at tennis
and still be serious about it.

Rod Laver

I like the creativity of tennis.

Guillermo Vilas

I play much better when I'm happy and having fun. That's common sense.

Jim Courier

The game is elementary.
Either the ball goes over the net or it doesn't,
lands inside the rectangle or outside it.

Bud Collins

To me tennis was more of an art
than a sport. Everything was done by impulse
or intuition. I'm a natural player who goes
along creating at the moment.

Maria Bueno

It is the beauty of the game ... it is the chase,
always, rather than the quarry.

Franklin P. Adams

Nothing in tennis is secure. There are the variables of the racket, the surface, the weather, the opponent, the spin and speed of the ball. Where you were. Who you were. For me, this is an unbelievable attraction.

Guillermo Vilas

On one day, off the next.
It's one of the fascinating things about tennis that nobody can figure out.

Roy Emerson

Tennis seems innocently simple to those who are outside the fence looking in.

Vic Braden

The minute you think you know all there is to know about tennis is the minute your game starts going down the tubes.

Jimmy Connors

Tennis is a perfect
combination of violent
action taking place
in an atmosphere
of total tranquillity.

Billie Jean King

Baseball is pursuing that hypnotic sound —
the crack of the bat on horsehide. With tennis,
it's the *puh!* of the strings on rubber.

Bud Collins

A tennis player can create more
than a painter.

Guillermo Vilas

I play for the love of the game. I think about
having fun and what a pleasure playing tennis
is. That seems to relax me and allows me
to concentrate on playing my best.

Evonne Goolagong

Tennis is the sport
for a lifetime.

Rod Laver

2

The Mental Game

Yogi Berra once observed, "Baseball is 90% mental and the other half physical." The same is true of tennis, only more so.

Winning tennis requires discipline, concentration and focus. In his fine book *The Inner Game of Tennis*, Dr. Timothy Gallwey writes, "Anxiety is fear about what may happen in the future, and it occurs only when the mind is imagining what the future may bring. But when attention is on the here and now, actions which need to be done have the best chance of being successfully accomplished."

If you're looking for prompt improvements on the court, begin by playing in the "here and now." Then brush up on the mental half of your game. Here's how.

Tennis begins off the court.

Brad Gilbert

To be a top tennis player you have to have a tough streak in you. I was ruthless and determined because I really wanted to win. It's good for women to have a tough streak, just like it's important for a guy to be sensitive.

Chris Evert

When you're put in a tough situation, you can't run from it — you have to deal with it. Otherwise, you lose.

Michael Chang

Be a sportsman, but have a killer instinct.

Bill Tilden

Tennis is a fight
of character.

Charlie Pasarell

Tennis is the strangest game ever.
It's all in your head. Little things can bother
you, destroy your game. So think
what a big thing can do.

Ilie Nastase

Believe in yourself.

Boris Becker

Every time you win, it diminishes the fear
a little bit. You never really cancel the fear
of losing; you keep challenging it.

Arthur Ashe

The players who have the most trouble
enjoying tennis are players who constantly
expect too much of themselves.

Rod Laver

When I play my best I just surge forward.
I try to play aggressively, and nerves
don't enter into it at all.

Chris Evert

Never give up. Repeat. Never give up.

Jimmy Connors

I can, *and I will!*

Helen Wills' Motto

Every time someone tells me I can't do
something, I tell myself I not only can,
but must.

Billie Jean King

Everything in this game
is within.

Arthur Ashe

The will to win is inside
you. You have
to bring it out.

Jimmy Connors

Most stress in tennis is really self-imposed.

Vic Braden

When calm alertness is maintained on the
tennis court, you are ready to perform
nearer the limit of your ability.

W. Timothy Gallwey

One must separate the emotional
from the practical.

Arthur Ashe

When you feel tense on the court,
utilize deep breathing.

Fred Stolle

The best players learn to use tension
generated by competition to bring out their
best tennis.

Fred Stolle

Relax physically between points. But never
relax mentally until the match is over.

Bill Tilden

Many of the difficulties in tennis are mental
in origin.

W. Timothy Gallwey

It's amazing how people can talk themselves
into something and then reinforce
a false opinion.

Arthur Ashe

Warm-ups begin with your *brain*.

Brad Gilbert

Confidence goes back and forth across
a tennis net much like the ball itself,
and only somewhat less frequently.

John McPhee

I played and won some long matches in front
of big crowds. It was my confidence that
grew first, and that helped my strokes.

Björn Borg

Don't just watch your opponent's strokes — watch his attitudes and habits.

Harry Hopman

Tennis and psychology are natural playmates.

Ethan Gologor

Everything you do of an athletic nature is
as much an extension of your personality
as it is a reflection of your particular
physical strengths and weaknesses.

Billie Jean King

The game that takes place in the mind is
played against such obstacles as lapses in
concentration, nervousness, self-doubt and
self-condemnation. In short, it is played to
overcome all habits of mind which inhibit
excellence in performance.

W. Timothy Gallwey

Early in your career, you're still trying
to prove something. In the last few years, I felt
I had to make every point. Eventually,
the pressure gets to you.

Louise Brough

You've got to get to that stage in your life
where going for it is more important
than winning or losing.

Arthur Ashe

The secret to winning any game lies
in not trying too hard.

W. Timothy Gallwey

A better game of tennis can coexist
with laughter — and it should.

Vic Braden

Pressure usually represents opportunity.

Jimmy Connors

Fortune favors the brave.

John Newcombe

The meek may inherit the earth, but they won't win many tennis matches.

Brad Gilbert

3

Practice

Vic Braden wrote, "If the pain you are suffering in losing to people is greater than the pain of making changes, then by all means, make the changes." His advice was straightforward and sensible, but easier said than done. Every tennis player knows that lasting changes are impossible to effect in the heat of battle. That's why quality practice is essential to winning tennis.

There is little glamour in long hours spent on the practice court, but the payoff is denominated in victories. If that payoff seems worth the price, consider the following advice.

Practice

Even when you're on top of your strokes,
maintain the quality of your game
with lessons.

Jimmy Connors

Everyone needs a coach, friend, or family
member who can see what you're doing
when you cannot see it.

Pete Sampras

The great champions are not born but
are made by their own — and at times
by their coaches' — efforts.

Bill Tilden

Most players don't take enough lessons.

Arthur Ashe

How does a good player become
a world-class player? Experience, hard work,
determination and concentration.

Harry Hopman

Practice. Eat. Sleep. Practice.

Boris Becker

No one becomes a successful player
without paying the price in practice.

Nick Bollettieri

Cut out the fancy thinking and just
concentrate on mastering the fundamentals,
and you'll beat most of the people
who now beat you.

Vic Braden

Most social tennis players could play a lot
better and enjoy themselves more in the
process if they would just solidify
their groundstrokes.

Rod Laver

The ultimate tactic in the game of tennis
is consistency. Consistency is your
most devastating weapon.

Bill Tym

The basic law of tennis: Learn to hit the same old boring winner.

Vic Braden

Most of us who aspire to be tops
in our field don't really consider the amount
of work required to stay tops.

Althea Gibson

The way to improve is to keep trying
through the down times. Keep trying and
keep banging on the door until it opens.

Nick Bollettieri

Champions keep playing
until they get it right.

Billie Jean King

Everybody advances at their own pace
in tennis.

Rod Laver

Progress and improvement do not come
in big bunches, they come in little pieces.

Arthur Ashe

Go slow, practice hard, work like a pack mule.

Ion Tiriac

Make the most of what you've got.
Brad Gilbert

The practice court should be used more
to practice weaknesses than strengths.
Harry Hopman

If you spend a half-hour on your forehand,
spend a half-hour on your backhand and
never, never run around either shot.
Billie Jean King

Playing serious tennis is hard work,
and there are no shortcuts to the top.
Stefan Edberg

There's always more to learn in this game,
no matter how long you've been playing.

Roy Emerson

I will overcome my weaknesses, *defeat* them.

Arthur Ashe

Perfect strokes are already in us, waiting
to be discovered.

W. Timothy Gallwey

Practice may not make things perfect,
but it sure makes things better.

Brad Gilbert

You can't expect to take a couple of lessons,
play a few sets, and then call yourself a tennis
player. You have to respect the difficulties
of the game if you want to enjoy yourself
from the start.

Roy Emerson

The best practice is done with a real partner
in conditions as close as possible
to a real tennis match.

Pancho Gonzales

An hour of hard practice is better than
three hours of going through the motions.

Pete Sampras

Five sets of singles in practice are equal
to three in a match.

Eleanor "Teach" Tennant

Try to find a mix of stronger and weaker
practice partners. Against the weaker players,
you can work on your weaknesses.
Against the stronger players,
you'll have to use your strengths.

Fred Stolle

Find a practice player who is as eager
as you are to improve his tennis.

Jimmy Connors

Never practice with anyone
who isn't serious about practicing.

Pancho Segura

In learning how to play tennis, the best thing
is to develop good habits before you've had
a chance to pick up bad ones.

Rod Laver

When I struggled within myself and had to
build myself up, I did it on the practice court.

Margaret Smith Court

The more serious you are about getting
good at tennis, the more serious you should
be about conditioning.

Rod Laver

Lendl had me biking twenty miles a day,
talking to me about discipline and working
hard and practicing until I couldn't walk
home. I'll never forget that.

Pete Sampras

My father was a strict disciplinarian.
He was a tough, demanding teacher and was
very critical of my play. I didn't have much fun
working, but his discipline was probably what
made me a champion.

Chris Evert

My father makes sure I don't play too much.
It's tough keeping my hands off a racket.

Steffi Graf

Practice the same shot over and over again
until mechanically it is almost instinctive.

Bill Tilden

If you're not willing to give 100 percent,
then it's time to get out. Forever.

Chris Evert

There's no excuse for a poor serve —
serving well is simply a matter of practice.

Pancho Gonzales

The serve is one shot you can work on
by yourself.

Bobby Riggs

The best way to master the serve is
to practice it by hitting against a fence. That
way you can perfect the basic motion before
you worry about putting the ball in.

Rod Laver

Improve your service return. You can turn
your opponent's serve into your advantage.

Jimmy Connors

You've got to push. You've got to act as though you expect a breakthrough to come tomorrow. But when you know it's not going to come, don't give up.

Arthur Ashe

Every match I ever won had been the result of practice and determination and hard work.

Angela Mortimer

Unless you're extremely gifted, there is no such thing as instant gratification in tennis.

Billie Jean King

Often after I lost a tournament, I'd be out practicing harder than ever to make up my mind I wasn't going to lose the next one.

Margaret Smith Court

Learn a lesson every time you lose.

John McEnroe

Work hard and
rest comes easy.

Nick Bollettieri

Spend more time preparing and less time regretting.

Virginia Wade

4

Concentration

The noted coach Harry Hopman observed, "The great qualities of a tennis champion are concentration, discipline, and dedication." It's no surprise that Hopman listed concentration first.

Great players learn to focus their physical and mental energies on the task at hand. They forget about past mistakes; they ignore impending peril. Instead, the best players give total concentration to the only point that matters: this one.

To be successful, a
certain single-mindedness
is required — on the
court or off.

Arthur Ashe

In tennis, concentration is vital to learning
the game — and once learned,
even more vital in playing it.

Bill Tilden

The day of the match I'm visualizing certain
points and my opponent's weaknesses and
strengths. I'm thinking, not chitchatting.

Chris Evert

All I ever see is my opponent.
You could set off dynamite in the next court,
and I wouldn't notice.

Maureen Connolly

I had one thought: to put the ball across
the net. I was simply myself, too deeply
concentrated on the game
for any extraneous thought.

Helen Wills

The secret of my success? Concentration.

Chris Evert

Concentration

The greatest lapses in concentration come
when we allow our minds to project what
is about to happen or dwell on what
has already happened.

W. Timothy Gallwey

I've been able to isolate points. Each point
I play is the "now moment."

Billie Jean King

On court, only think about winning
the next point.

John McEnroe

When I was playing my best, I was never
aware of the people, the fans. All I wanted
was to win.

Ilie Nastase

Keep your mind, above all,
on the bloody ball.

Roy Emerson

Take good care of the shot you're on — it's probably your last one on this point.

Vic Braden

You can overcome tennis nerves
by not dwelling so much on the risk of losing.

Arthur Ashe

Play inside the lines.
Don't let outside distractions bother you.
Keep your concentration.

Pete Sampras

When you lose your temper, you lose
your concentration.

Rod Laver

Anger out of control kills you.
Anger for the right reason helps you.

Brad Gilbert

If there's one thing you *don't* want
to concentrate on, it's the point you just lost.

Roy Emerson

Thinking about past points you lost only costs you future points.

Bill Tilden

Concentration isn't something
that comes naturally.

Roy Emerson

When I am within a point or two of losing
a game, I *do* feel very determined and
remember that I must keep
a strict command over myself.

Charlotte "Lottie" Dod, 1887

Concentrate hard on the big points to give
yourself every chance of making a great shot.
The ability to hit great shots in a crisis
has made national champions out of many
players with quite ordinary strokes.

Rod Laver

Concentrate without *trying* to concentrate.

W. Timothy Gallwey

There is the need for mental stamina —
the ability to stay alert when everything in
you cries out for mental and physical repose.

Rex Bellamy

You want a combination of single-minded
focus and relaxed muscles.

Stan Smith

To stay concentrated between points, focus
attention on the natural rhythm of breathing.

W. Timothy Gallwey

I believe that the champion will miss almost
as many shots as the second-class player,
but he will miss them at different times.
The champion seldom misses a shot he
should make at a crucial moment.

Bill Tilden

Build your game based upon taking the high percentage shot and knowing how to execute that shot under pressure.

Vic Braden

The tennis ball has a quality which makes it a very good object for concentration: It is moving. The mind is attracted by objects in motion; it has been ever since birth.

W. Timothy Gallwey

You have to work at concentration the same way you have to work on your strokes and your stamina.

Roy Emerson

You hear a lot of talk in this game about reflexes, but what passes for quick reflexes is often nothing more than good concentration.

Rod Laver

Good concentration separates champions from almost-champions.

Stan Smith

5

The Serve

In tennis, everything starts with a serve: This is the shot that begins every point of every game of every match. No wonder all serious players are serious about their service game.

Powerful servers are impressive to watch. But the most effective shot is not always the fastest; placement and consistency are often more important than speed. As Pancho Segura warned, "Losers have cannonball first serves and soft ball second serves."

In this chapter, some of the game's great masters share their tips. If you follow their advice, you'll experience something that every tennis player craves: service with a smile.

Your service usually determines whether you will win or lose the match.

Pancho Gonzales

In tennis, the serve offers the one opportunity
to control everything.

Pancho Gonzales

Controlling the serve
is everybody's problem.

Rod Laver

In tennis, the server is given a tremendous
advantage. Don't throw this advantage away.

Harry Hopman

The hardest stroke in tennis to learn,
and the most important, is the serve.

Rod Laver

Service, above all other shots, is a matter
of practice, practice, and more practice.

Bill Tilden

The best service model to follow is
Pancho Gonzales. Everyone can learn
from his deliberate motion.

Roy Emerson

A serve does not have to be powerful
to be effective.

Françoise Durr

All great services are hit with ease,
simplicity, and apparently little
body movement.

Bill Tilden

On the serve, generate power
through rhythm rather than brute force.

Vic Braden

Let the serve serve itself.

W. Timothy Gallwey

Whenever I try to hit hard, I serve slow. When I don't worry about speed, but about the serve quality, I serve fast.

Goran Ivanisevic

I feel empathy for the weekend player when he has service problems and can't figure out where he's gone wrong. Here I am, supposedly one of the best three or four servers in the whole bloody world, and I don't know what I'm doing wrong.

Arthur Ashe

In serving, it's the toss that gets most people in trouble.

Roy Emerson

When the toss is off, it throws the whole rhythm haywire. When you lose that groove, you start to struggle and expend a great deal more energy.

Arthur Ashe

What gets most beginners in trouble? The toss.

Bill Tilden

Rushing the serve is the biggest mistake
    players at every level of the game make,
    particularly after they miss the first serve.

Roy Emerson

Serve to your opponent's weakness.

Billie Jean King

The basic principle should be: Always serve
    to the shot which will produce the highest
    and weakest ball in return. Usually, that shot
    is your opponent's backhand.

Vic Braden

If your serve is working well for you,
    it usually shows up in the rest of your game.

Roy Emerson

Eliminate frustration, and you will find
    yourself serving accurately.

W. Timothy Gallwey

The one luxury you have on the serve that
you don't have on any other stroke is that you
can control the pace by yourself.

Roy Emerson

Your first serve should go in 70% of the time.

Pancho Gonzales

A big serve will start to look fat
if you don't move it around.

Brad Gilbert

No matter what the quality of your opponent,
keep him or her off balance by varying
the speed, twist and spin of your serve.

Françoise Durr

The time you're most likely to lose your
serve is right after you've broken serve.

Brad Gilbert

The most important percentage shot
in tennis is the second serve.

Jack Kramer

You never see a top-notch match where the
depth and accuracy of the second serve
is not a factor.

Jack Kramer

With the serve, unless you get the bloody
thing in, it doesn't matter how hard you hit it.

Rod Laver

When serving, remember that depth
is more important than speed.

Billie Jean King

Losers serve double-faults.

Pancho Segura

The serve was invented so the net can play.

Bill Cosby

6

Strokes

Bill Tilden wrote, "Strokes are the weapons with which you fight your tennis battles. The better your weapons, the greater your chance of victory." Big Bill knew lots about victory; he was the greatest player of his age.

Few of us will ever reach the Hall of Fame, but all of us can improve our strokes. We do so through instruction and repetition.

If you're intent upon upgrading *your* tennis weapons, find a good instructor and groove your swing in practice. Then, hit a few million shots for good measure. You'll discover that, on the tennis court, your weapons will take good care of you if you take good care of them.

The solutions to developing sound strokes aren't in far-out theories; they're inside *you*.

Vic Braden

As tennis players, we tend to think too much before and during our shots; we try too hard to control our movements; and we are too concerned about the results of our actions.

W. Timothy Gallwey

You get a great feeling when you're hitting the ball really well. The ball comes over the net looking as big as a soccer ball, and everything seems to be moving in slow motion. You feel as if there's nothing you can't do with the ball. You get confidence. You're loose, relaxed. Everything is working for you.

Rod Laver

Consistency is a mental weapon.

Nick Bollettieri

Be patient. Don't force a shot
that isn't there.

Ivan Lendl

Every time you make an unforced error,
you take the pressure off the other player and
put it on yourself.

Rod Laver

Good strokes help you relax as you play.

Vic Braden

If you see a tennis player who looks
like he is working hard, then that means
he isn't very good.

Helen Wills

Never wait for the ball to arrive. This isn't the Post Office. You don't wait for delivery.

Brad Gilbert

The secret of preparation for a shot lies
in taking the racquet head back *the moment*
you see where the shot is coming.

Bill Tilden

Since your goal is never to be rushed
on your swing, it's impossible to be too early
on your backswing.

Vic Braden

The reason Chris Evert hardly ever
misses from the baseline is that her feet are
always in good position for a smooth stroke.

Rod Laver

Work hard on getting to the ball early
so that you can be absolutely calm
as you take your swing.

Vic Braden

Strokes

Footwork is the most important part
of the game. It's everything.

Brad Gilbert

When you play a better player, don't try
to hit harder. Play your own game, but try
to be faster on your feet.

Pancho Gonzales

Get happy feet, not heavy feet.

Brad Gilbert

The more I see of great champions, the more
I feel they have two common denominators:
foot speed and the ability to hit topspin.

Jack Kramer

No matter what your ability or strength —
or what you have been told — you can learn
to hit topspin.

Vic Braden

Make it a point to find your ideal point
of contact. It's different from mine
or any other player's.

Stan Smith

Try to watch the ball all the way to the point
of contact without turning your head
drastically.

Stan Smith

It's amazing how many errors occur
in a professional match because one of the
players simply takes his eye off the ball.

Rod Laver

Agility is the key to good volleying.
Agility, confidence, and aggressiveness.

Roy Emerson

The strokes that are prettiest in the warm-up
are the ugliest under pressure.

Brad Gilbert

Basically, a good tennis player can be
defined as one who is able to hit a target area
while under stress.

Vic Braden

The best advice I can give the student
of stroke technique is *keep it simple,
keep it natural.*

W. Timothy Gallwey

I get into trouble when I try to put too much
muscle into the volley — especially the
backhand volley. The best way is to hit it
short, quick and strong, like a pistol shot.

Rod Laver

You must curb any desire to hit everything
with power.

Harry Hopman

Pressure is the ultimate lie detector. That's when strokes speak the truth.

Brad Gilbert

The ground strokes are the most fundamental shots of tennis, and the most important.

Billie Jean King

Without a reliable volley, you can't be an aggressive player. A good volley allows you to take charge of a point.

Tony Trabert

With a volley, you're blocking the ball, not stroking it.

Rod Laver

With the volley, time it well and hit it cleanly. The less arm the better.

Roy Emerson

When you hit the high backhand volley, don't be timid. Think John Wayne.

Roy Emerson

If you're trying to improve your net game,
  watching Wimbledon is almost like getting
two weeks of lessons on how to play the net.

Tim Gullikson

To visualize hitting through the ball, think of
a defensive halfback in football intercepting a
pass on the run. If he times the interception
well, he doesn't even break stride. That's how
  most tennis strokes should be hit.

Rod Laver

In terms of hitting a ball on a horizontal
  plane, the net is very high. So think of *lifting*
    the ball over a high barrier.

Vic Braden

If your backhand is your strongest stroke,
    you'll never break down. Never.

Dr. Robert Walter Johnson

A couple of good shots
can make you forget
all the lousy ones.

Rod Laver

7

Strategy

As Rod Laver observed, "Tennis is a game of pressure: the object is to keep the pressure on the other player so that he'll make an error sooner or later, and to keep the pressure off yourself." But how does one best manage the pressures of tennis? By thinking ahead.

Players who simply bang away and hope are usually closed out in straight sets. But players who think their way around the court enjoy a powerful, winning advantage.

In this chapter we examine the principles of sound tennis strategy. Thankfully, these principles are straightforward: Keep the ball in play, hit it deep, attack when you can, and always keep up the pressure — on the other guy.

The first rule of tennis tactics: Keep the ball
in play and give your opponent another shot
rather than taking an unnecessary chance.

Bill Tilden

The first major rule for any tennis player:
Get the ball back into the other person's court.

Don Budge

The good percentage player takes
one chance per point.

Tony Trabert

Whether you're serving or receiving,
if you hit the ball in five times, you won't lose
any matches.

Arthur Ashe

Force your opponent to hit to your strength
or make an error.

Nick Bollettieri

Force your opponent to beat you
with his weaker shots.

Vic Braden

Don't beat yourself with unnecessary
errors. Hit offensive or defensive shots
depending on the situation.

Rod Laver

Your primary consideration in shot selection
is to attempt only those shots you know
you can make.

Bill Tym

Let your opponent make the mistakes.

Father's Advice to Chris Evert

Don't force shots. Don't get impatient.
Don't try to make something out of nothing.
Play like a boa constrictor. Just keep squeezing.

Brad Gilbert

The primary object in match tennis
is to break up the other man's game.

Bill Tilden

Decide what feature of your opponent's
game you will attempt to exploit,
and then hop on it.

Bill Tilden

Never allow your opponent to play
the game he prefers if you can force him
to play any other.

Bill Tilden

Probe. Put pressure on your opponent's weaknesses.

John McEnroe

The key to tactical success in tennis
is control. Keep the ball in play longer than
your opponent, and you're going to win.

Roy Emerson

Good shot selection is the cornerstone
of a tactically sound game. *Where* and *when*
you hit a shot is more important
than *how* you hit it.

Bill Tym

The key to raising your game successfully
is to play within yourself. Don't try shots
you would have to be lucky to make.

Arthur Ashe

Never try to hit a shot you don't "own".

Vic Braden

Make your opponent beat you at what you do best.

Stefan Edberg

The percentage shot in tennis is the shot that strikes the balance between the pressure you're putting on yourself to make a testing shot and the pressure you're putting on the other player to make a good return.

Rod Laver

Be patient, but move your opponent around until you get a short ball you can move in and hit with a little extra juice.

Nick Bollettieri

Attack when you've got the opportunity, but don't be guilty of overkill.

Roy Emerson

My philosophy is that every swing you take should progress the rally in your favor.

Andre Agassi

If you can learn to hit the ball deep and down the middle — and keep it in play — that's all the strategy you'll need to beat 99 percent of the players in the world.

Vic Braden

Depth is the byword of successful percentage tennis.

Tony Trabert

Keeping the ball in play and keeping it deep will inevitably lead to errors by your opponent.

Nick Bollettieri

Hit deep early.

Brad Gilbert

Keep all your shots deep and in play and you'll be famous by Friday.

Vic Braden

The basics of percentage tennis can be
summarized in three principles:
  1. Keep the ball in play.
  2. Keep the ball deep.
  3. Attack the short ball.

Nick Bollettieri

The basic principles for successful doubles
play are quite simple:
  1. Keep the ball in play.
  2. Play together as a team.
  3. Attack!

Rod Laver and Roy Emerson

Don't try to do too much when hitting from
your weaker side. Use your weaker shot
to keep the ball in play.

Tony Trabert

If you've lost a long set,
change something immediately.

Ethan Gologor

On a slow surface, a serve-and-volley game
alone isn't enough. You have to be consistent
from the baseline, and you have to be patient.

Roy Emerson

Pro doubles teams talk to each other
an average of 83 times during a match.

Dr. Jim Loehr

In tennis, you practically always have
the option of making a conservative shot or a
risky one. The game is unique for allowing
that possibility continually.

Ethan Gologor

On most shots, it's easier to lose the point
by making an error than it is to win it
by hitting an outright winner.

Rod Laver

Perfect back play will beat perfect volleying.

Herbert F. Lawford, 1887

Make your opponent move as much as
possible. When you've got him on a string —
you've got him.

Tony Trabert

Tennis is giving your opponent one more
chance to run out of gas.

Jack Kramer

8

Winning and Losing

Maureen Connolly, the first woman to win tennis' Grand Slam, was poetic in describing her game. She said, "I have always believed greatness on a tennis court was my destiny, a dark destiny at times, where the tennis court became my secret jungle and I, a lonely, fear-stricken hunter."

The court *can* be a jungle, especially when one is paired against an imposing opponent. In this chapter, we set out in search of winning secrets. Happy hunting.

Never change a winning game; always change a losing one.

Bill Tilden

You win alone, just as you lose alone.

Arthur Ashe

I hate to lose more than I like to win. I hate
to see the happiness on their faces
when they beat me.

Jimmy Connors

Sometimes, a tennis match comes down to a
battle of the minds. The player who hangs
in longer, wins.

Chris Evert

Winning breeds winning.

Pete Sampras

Champions take responsibility. When the
ball is coming over the net, you can be sure
I want the ball.

Billie Jean King

Pressure your opponent when you're ahead.

Ivan Lendl

It's truly a great player who gets hungrier
with a lead.

Brad Gilbert

A tennis player must go after her opponent
as a cat goes after a mouse.

Karolj Seles (Monica's father)

I am really happy when the last point is over
in a tournament and I have won. Five minutes
later, however, it's all gone.

Arthur Ashe

Don't have your victory party before you
have your victory.

Brad Gilbert

When you're losing, some strategy,
  even though it may be the wrong strategy,
    is better than no strategy.

Ethan Gologor

Most of the time there is a way to win.
  You just have to figure out what it is.

Brad Gilbert

In its process of developing, our tennis game
  learns a great deal from errors.

W. Timothy Gallwey

I loved to win, and I liked being at the top.
  When I lost, it normally made me much more
    determined to get up and show them
      that I could do it.

Margaret Smith Court

No one's ever given me anything on the court.
  Maybe that's one reason I prefer singles.
It's just me and you. When I win, I don't have
  to congratulate anyone. When I lose,
    I don't have to blame anyone.

Jimmy Connors

As you stay on the top longer, there is more pressure building up. You get to the point where you're just playing not to lose.

Louise Brough

After a defeat, the press makes me feel as if I'm on trial.

Arthur Ashe

A champion is forever under scrutiny.

Don Budge

Defeat is always hardest for me the next day, because it stays with me and swells.

Arthur Ashe

You just *have* to care — about anything
you have to do. You appreciate excellence
for excellence's sake.

Arthur Ashe

In true competition, no person is defeated.
Both players benefit by their efforts to overcome the obstacles presented by the other.

W. Timothy Gallwey

Everybody must learn to lose. You can't
play the game if you can't take the losing.

Arthur Ashe

I like to go on court now knowing it's not the
end of the world if I lose.

Virginia Wade

The moment of victory
is much too short to live
for that and nothing else.

Martina Navratilova

Part of the fun of the game
        is overcoming difficulties.

Rod Laver

Forget about your losses. Laugh and hit. You'll
have more fun and win more in the long run.

Vic Braden

There's no such thing as a bad sport.
    You're either a sport or you're not a sport.

Margaret Osborne duPont

When you're winning — or losing —
        keep success in perspective.

Chris Evert

There is no way you can remind yourself
        too much that tennis is only a game,
            just a bloody game.

Roy Emerson

Too great a degree of importance is placed
on victory, either for the money, the prestige,
the club, or the country.

Jean Borotra

Be gracious in both victory and defeat.

Rod Laver

If you can react the same way to winning
or to losing, that's a big accomplishment.

Chris Evert

Tennis became easier once I realized I was
putting too much emphasis on winning.

Michael Chang

There is no disgrace in defeat.
Champions are born in the labor of defeat.

Bill Tilden

If, with God's help,
I cannot beat my
opponent, I accept
defeat as something
that was ordained.

Althea Gibson

Never equate losing with failure.

Arthur Ashe

<u>9</u>

Life

The game of tennis has lessons to teach which extend far beyond the court. In fact, the most valuable tennis lessons have nothing to do with serves, volleys, overheads or lobs; the most valuable lessons teach us about life. On the pages that follow, notable players and coaches share their insights about the game played outside the lines.

When I was working up to the top,
    those were happy days.

Louise Brough

I enjoyed the struggling years much more.

Pauline Betz

I know that I would hate life if I were
deprived of trying, hunting, working for some
objective within which there lies the beauty
of perfection.

Helen Wills

Working hard and trying to be your best:
That's what tennis and life have in common
for me.

Chris Evert

If my plane goes down tomorrow, I don't want to be the richest guy in the cemetery. I want to go down in a good mood.

Ilie Nastase

Whatever I do, I like to stop and sniff the flowers.

Evonne Goolagong

Glory is often worth the price one pays for it.

Charles Lenglen (Suzanne's father)

Conscience is more important than money.

Charlie Pasarell

I am blessed with a talent, and I have an obligation to the Lord to make the most of it.

Andre Agassi

You have within you the power to make tennis fun, to build confidence, and to play consistently. The result is a higher quality of both tennis and life.

Steve Wilkinson

Welcoming obstacles in competition automatically increases the ability to find advantage in all the difficulties one meets in the course of one's life.

W. Timothy Gallwey

I used to put so much emphasis on tennis. But now I've learned that the great things in life are the simple, basic things.

Chris Evert

Many times one feels oneself to be secure, and suddenly, one's world falls down like a pack of cards in a matter of seconds.

Guillermo Vilas

Remember: There is always the possibility that some good will arise from an unfortunate situation.

Arthur Ashe

The last point means nothing, the next point means nothing. All that counts in the whole world is this now point, and that's where I'm living for all I'm worth. Now.

Billie Jean King

Tennis is a great game, and I'd love to win every match I play, but it's not the ultimate thing in life.

Pete Sampras

I can get very determined when I'm playing, but I never wanted tennis to be everything.

Evonne Goolagong

There will be other tennis matches.

Helen Wills

We have to live for today and not worry about or try to know what tomorrow brings.

Monica Seles

If I had my life to live
over — I would be
a topspin player.

Françoise Durr

You can't change the last point, so forget it. Win the next one.

Rod Laver

10

All-Purpose Advice

La Rochefoucauld observed, "We give nothing so freely as advice." Nowhere are these words more true than on the tennis court. When it comes to tennis tips, everyone, it seems, is an expert.

In this chapter, we consider *good* advice on a variety of tennis topics. Although freely given, it is well worth following.

Play high-percentage tennis. Make your
opponent earn every bloody point!

Rod Laver

Wait for the opportunity to put your
best shots into use.

Rod Laver

Don't go for the big shot when you
don't need it!

Pancho Gonzales

Start with steadiness and smarts.
Then add aggression and power.

Arthur Ashe

Before you learn tactics, learn ball control.

Pancho Segura

I believe in always hitting the ball with all my might, but there seems to be a disposition to "just get it over" in many girls whom I have played. I do not call this tennis.

Molla Mallory, 1920

Don't try for winners on every shot. Wait for the right moment.

Bobby Riggs

Let's face it: The most glamorous part of any game is the offense. But defense is the key to victory. So keep plugging away and get the ball back.

Bobby Riggs

When you've got an opponent down, slam the door by going with your best strokes and best plan.

Jimmy Connors

Simplify everything you do right down
to the bare essentials.

Billie Jean King

Simplicity is the key to consistency.

W. Timothy Gallwey

My biggest strength is that I don't have
any weaknesses.

John McEnroe

Remember that the net is an even bigger
obstacle than your opponent. Most of your
errors will end up in the net.

Rod Laver

Never take your eye off the ball in order
to watch your opponent.

Rod Laver

Watch the ball come off
your opponent's racket.

Pancho Gonzales

When you're returning a serve,
watch the ball, not your opponent.

Don Budge

Watch the ball as though it might disappear
at any moment.

Pancho Gonzales

In working with beginners,
I repeat this instruction
thirty times an hour:
Keep your eye on the ball.

Bill Tilden

Don't sit in the sun before matches, or you'll
be tired before you walk on the court.

Vic Braden

Get into the habit of starting out slowly.
The warm-up is important not just for the
now-and-then player.

Rod Laver

Run when very tired.
Stretch when very cold.

Ion Tiriac

Don't wait to drink water until your
tongue's hanging out. You wouldn't wait to fill
up your gas tank until you ran out of gas.

Brad Gilbert

I take my time and don't show a lot of
emotion on the court because I don't want to
waste energy, and I don't want my opponents
to see how I really feel.

Chris Evert

Anger doesn't help you play better.

Rod Laver

Don't argue about the marginal call.
But don't let a blatantly bad call go by
without action.

Brad Gilbert

If you're not sure if a ball is in or out,
give your opponent a reasonable benefit
of the doubt.

Rod Laver

Set your own tempo. Do it courteously, with
all due regard for your opponent's "rights,"
but do it.

Bill Tilden

I pray, but I don't pray
to win. I pray for the
inspiration to give
my best.

Althea Gibson

In every match, there is one overriding fact:
You are you. So know yourself.

Rod Laver

Work with what you have.

Roy Emerson

Be moral, be ethical, work hard, and don't
pay too much attention to the critics.

Nick Bollettieri

Winners look like winners. Exude a confident
image, even if you don't feel confident.

Stan Smith

A champion always attaches to herself
an aura of ascendancy.

Ann Haydon Jones

Keep your excuses
to yourself and give
your opponent credit
for success.

Harry Hopman

<u>11</u>

Observations on Love, Lobs, and Other Facts of Tennis Life

We conclude with a potpourri of insights and advice. Enjoy!

Tennis helps me keep my sanity.

Billie Jean King

The whole point of my tennis is that I have
always loved playing the game.

Virginia Wade

If I had one wish to bequeath to the game
it would be to sometimes have
a little laughter on court.

Laurie Pignon

Play tennis without fear of defeat
and because it's fun, or don't play at all.

Bill Tilden

I can live without the crowds and publicity. But I have to play, and I always will, even if it's at a public park with nobody watching.

Billie Jean King

D on't be a prisoner of tennis.
Have balance in your life.

Monica Seles

The best tennis advice I can ever give is this: Keep the game fun.

Jimmy Connors

I urge you — play tennis! Tennis is the most valuable sport that any individual can learn, even more so than golf.

Bill Tilden

A Top 20 player who wins the first set
will go on to win the match 89.6 percent
of the time.

Association of Tennis Professionals

Good tennis is not necessarily synonymous
with belting the ball. It is making
the right stroke at the right time.

Harry Hopman

A badly produced shot to the right place
is always better than the most beautiful shot
in the world to the wrong place.

Bill Tilden

Lob more.

Rod Laver

No matter how many adjustments you
   might make in your swing, a proper grip
      will last for the rest of your life.

Vic Braden

Sometimes I lose early, then next week I
beat everybody. Consistency comes with age.

A Young Boris Becker

I know a lot of intermediate players who
   change rackets like television channels.
   A new racket comes out... they'll buy it,
      thinking it's going to make a world of
difference in their game. It usually doesn't.

Rod Laver

The minute you get a little tentative
on the overhead, you might as well not hit it.

Roy Emerson

Players who move well, who swing smoothly
and with fluency and use their body weight
well, who don't fight their bodies when they
meet the ball — these are the players
who hardly ever get injured.

Roy Emerson

I just throw dignity to the winds and think
of nothing but the game.

Suzanne Lenglen

It can be very difficult to play doubles
with your spouse.

Chris Evert

Death is nature's way of giving somebody else
your tennis court.

Johnny Carson

Tennis etiquette is really nothing more than showing the same consideration to the people around you that you expect yourself.

Rod Laver

The polite manners of the game, that seemed so silly to me at first, gradually began to appeal to me. I began to understand that you could walk out on the court like a lady, all dressed up in immaculate white, be polite to everybody, and still play like a tiger.

Althea Gibson

Etiquette assumes importance in the making of calls. My philosophy, ever since I started playing, has been to give the other guy the benefit of the doubt on close calls.

Roy Emerson

There is a temptation to win by any means, and when that happens, it is the finish of sport.

Jean Borotra

Sportsmanship is the essence of the game.

Rod Laver

Recreational players are usually long
on running and short on thinking.

Brad Gilbert

A tennis player is like a Swiss watch.
There are 250 little wheels inside, and if one
is not working properly, you have a problem.

Ion Tiriac

There are four things players easily fall
prey to: poor preparation, overconfidence,
lousy shot selection, and nerves.

Brad Gilbert

The windmill contortionist is an eyesore
on the tennis courts.

Bill Tilden

My advice to young players is to see
as much good tennis as possible and then
attempt to copy the outstanding strokes
of the former stars.

Bill Tilden

Tips are a dime a dozen. What is difficult
is a workable way to apply tips, to replace
one pattern of behavior with a new one.

W. Timothy Gallwey

I think believing in yourself has a lot to do
with the words. You are what you say you are.
Your children will be what you say they are.
Words are important and powerful.

Margaret Smith Court

When you lose your confidence,
everything else goes.

Ilie Nastase

You don't need to get fancy. The better
you play, the more simplistic you become
in your approach to the game.

Vic Braden

Good balance means good control.
I've always figured that a person who's had
a lot of ballet training would make
a good tennis player.

Roy Emerson

The big difference between the very good
player and the average player is the ability to
"read" the ball as it's coming over the net.
The spin of the ball, the pace on it...
where you have to move to, *how fast* you
have to swing, and *what* you have to do
with the racket.

Roy Emerson

Tennis matches are won or lost by the sum
total of physical condition, courage,
intelligence, experience and stroke.
Luck plays practically no part
in the results of tennis matches.

Bill Tilden

The better one plays tennis, the greater
its rewards — materially, spiritually and
psychologically.

Bill Tilden

My only regrets are that I didn't try harder.

Louise Brough

After it's over, you can't bring a match back,
but you *can* learn from it.

Rod Laver

The only possible regret I have is the feeling that I will die without having played enough tennis.

Jean Borotra

Sources

Franklin P. Adams 18

Andre Agassi 98, 118

Arthur Ashe 26, 28, 31, 32, 35, 40, 44, 47, 53,
    58, 62, 74, 92, 96, 105, 106, 108, 109, 114,
    119, 124

Boris Becker 26, 41, 140

Rex Bellamy 65

Yogi Berra 23

Pauline Betz 116

Nick Bollettieri 42, 44, 55, 80, 92, 98, 99, 100,
    133

Björn Borg 32

Jean Borotra 112, 142, 148

Vic Braden 19, 30, 35, 39, 42, 43, 61, 66, 72, 75,
    80, 81, 83, 84, 86, 89, 93, 96, 99, 111, 130,
    140, 146

Louise Brough 35, 108, 116, 147

Don Budge 92, 108, 128

Maria Bueno 18

Johnny Carson 141

Michael Chang 24, 112

Bud Collins 18, 21

Maureen Connolly 59, 103

Jimmy Connors 19, 27, 29, 36, 40, 49, 52, 105,
    107, 126, 137

Bill Cosby 78

Jim Courier 17

Margaret Smith Court 50, 53, 107

Charlotte "Lottie" Dod 64

Margaret Osborne duPont 111

Françoise Durr 72, 76, 121

Stefan Edberg 46, 97

Roy Emerson 19, 47, 48, 60, 62, 64, 66, 72, 74,
    75, 76, 85, 88, 96, 98, 100, 101, 111, 133,
    140, 141, 142, 146

Chris Evert 24, 27, 51, 59, 105, 111, 112, 116,
    118, 131, 141

W. Timothy Gallwey 23, 31, 32, 34, 35, 47, 60,
    64, 65, 66, 72, 75, 80, 86, 107, 109, 118, 127,
    145

Althea Gibson 44, 113, 132, 142

Brad Gilbert 24, 32, 38, 46, 47, 62, 76, 82, 84,
    86, 87, 93, 99, 106, 107, 130, 131, 144

Ethan Gologor 34, 101, 102, 107

Pancho Gonzales 48, 52, 70, 71, 76, 84, 124,
    128

Evonne Goolagong 21, 117, 120

Steffi Graf 51

Tim Gullikson 89

Harry Hopman 33, 40, 46, 57, 71, 86, 134, 138

Goran Ivanisevic 73

Dr. Robert Walter Johnson 89

Ann Haydon Jones 133
Billie Jean King 15, 20, 27, 34, 44, 46, 53, 60,
    75, 77, 88, 105, 120, 127, 136, 137
Jack Kramer 77, 84, 102
La Rochefoucauld 123
Rod Laver 16, 22, 26, 42, 44, 50, 52, 62, 64, 67,
    71, 77, 80, 81, 83, 85, 86, 88, 89, 90, 91, 93,
    98, 100, 102, 111, 112, 122, 124, 127, 128,
    130, 131, 133, 139, 140, 142, 143, 147
Herbert F. Lawford 102
Ivan Lendl 81, 106
Charles Lenglen 117
Suzanne Lenglen 141
Dr. Jim Loehr 101
Molla Mallory 126
John McEnroe 54, 60, 95, 127
John McPhee 32
Angela Mortimer 53
Ilie Nastase 26, 60, 117, 145
Martina Navratilova 110
John Newcombe 37
Yannick Noah 16
Charlie Pasarell 25, 117
Laurie Pignon 136
Bobby Riggs 52, 126
Pete Sampras 40, 48, 50, 62, 105, 120

Pancho Segura 49, 69, 77, 125
Karolj Seles 106
Monica Seles 16, 120, 137
Stan Smith 65, 68, 85, 133
Fred Stolle 31, 49
Eleanor "Teach" Tennant 48
Bill Tilden 24, 31, 40, 51, 59, 63, 65, 71, 72, 74, 79, 83, 92, 94, 104, 112, 129, 131, 136, 137, 138, 144, 145, 147
Ion Tiriac 45, 130, 144
Tony Trabert 88, 92, 99, 101, 102
Bill Tym 42, 93, 96
Guillermo Vilas 16, 19, 21, 118
Virginia Wade 56, 109, 136
Steve Wilkinson 118
Helen Wills 27, 59, 81, 116, 120

WG

About the Author

Criswell Freeman is a Doctor of Clinical Psychology living in Nashville, Tennessee. He is the author of *When Life Throws You a Curveball, Hit It* and *The Wisdom Series* from WALNUT GROVE PRESS.

About Wisdom Books

Wisdom Books chronicle memorable quotations in an easy-to-read style. Written by Criswell Freeman, this series provides inspiring, thoughtful and humorous messages from entertainers, athletes, scientists, politicians, clerics, writers and renegades. Each title focuses on a particular region or area of special interest.

Combining his passion for quotations with extensive training in psychology, Dr. Freeman revisits timeless themes such as perseverance, courage, love, forgiveness and faith.

"Quotations help us remember the simple yet profound truths that give life perspective and meaning," notes Freeman. "When it comes to life's most important lessons, we can all use gentle reminders."

The Wisdom Series
by Dr. Criswell Freeman

Regional Titles

Wisdom Made in America	ISBN 1-887655-07-7
The Book of Southern Wisdom	ISBN 0-9640955-3-X
The Wisdom of the Midwest	ISBN 1-887655-17-4
The Wisdom of the West	ISBN 1-887655-31-X
The Book of Texas Wisdom	ISBN 0-9640955-8-0
The Book of Florida Wisdom	ISBN 0-9640955-9-9
The Book of California Wisdom	ISBN 1-887655-14-X
The Book of New York Wisdom	ISBN 1-887655-16-6
The Book of New England Wisdom	ISBN 1-887655-15-8

Sports Titles

The Golfer's Book of Wisdom	ISBN 0-9640955-6-4
The Putter Principle	ISBN 1-887655-39-5
The Golfer's Guide to Life	ISBN 1-887655-38-7
The Wisdom of Southern Football	ISBN 0-9640955-7-2
The Book of Stock Car Wisdom	ISBN 1-887655-12-3
The Wisdom of Old-Time Baseball	ISBN 1-887655-08-5
The Book of Football Wisdom	ISBN 1-887655-18-2
The Book of Basketball Wisdom	ISBN 1-887655-32-8
The Fisherman's Guide to Life	ISBN 1-887655-30-1
The Tennis Lover's Guide to Life	ISBN 1-887655-36-0

Special Interest Titles

The Book of Country Music Wisdom	ISBN 0-9640955-1-3
Old-Time Country Wisdom	ISBN 1-887655-26-3
The Wisdom of Old-Time Television	ISBN 1-887655-64-6
The Cowboy's Guide to Life	ISBN 1-887655-41-7
The Wisdom of the Heart	ISBN 1-887655-34-4
The Guide to Better Birthdays	ISBN 1-887655-35-2
The Gardener's Guide to Life	ISBN 1-887655-40-9
Minutes from the Great Women's Coffee Club (by Angela Beasley)	ISBN 1-887655-33-6